Friends for Life

For Wesley

A collection of words about
friendship featuring
the illustrations
of Rebecca Gryspeerdt

NEW YORK • WATFORD UK

'Friendship maketh daylight in the understanding out of the darkness and confusion of thought.'
FRANCIS BACON

'If I don't have friends, then I ain't got nothin.'
BILLY HOLIDAY

'Friendship is the gift of the gods, and the most precious boon to man.'
BENJAMIN DISRAELI

"Friendship comes in all sizes, colours and ways." IRMA

"Hold a true friend with both your hands."

NIGERIAN PROVERB

'A true friend is like the refrain of a beautiful song.'
F. PATARCA

'Friendship makes music a thousand times more sweet.'
HENRY VAN DYKE

'Friends do not live in harmony merely, as some say, but in melody.'
HENRY DAVID THOREAU

'Your friend is the person who knows all about you, and still likes you.'

ELBERT HUBBARD

'All the world is queer save thee and me. And even thou art a little queer.'

ROBERT OWEN

'The best rule of friendship is to keep your heart a little softer than your head.'

GEORGE SANTAYANA

'It is the friends you can call up
at 4 a.m. that matter.'
MARLENE DIETRICH

'What sunshine is to flowers, smiles are to humanity.'
JOSEPH ADDISON

'Friendship is like the sun's eternal face.'

JOHN GAY

'We have been friends together in sunshine and shade.'

CAROLINE NORTON

'A friend may well be reckoned the masterpiece of Nature.'

RALPH WALDO EMERSON

'True friendship comes when silence between two people is comfortable.'
DAVE TYSON GENTRY

'Silences make the real conversations between friends. Not the saying but the never needing to say is what counts.'
MARGARET LEE RUNBECK

'Silences and distances are woven into the texture of every true friendship.'
ROBERT ISRAEL

5 | SILENCES AND DISTANCES

'friendship is a plant
of slow growth.'
GEORGE WASHINGTON

' If you ever leave me ... ... I'm coming with you.' NAOMI JUDD

'If you accompany a friend, there is no detour too far.'
LEO TOLSTOY

'Kind words can be short and easy to speak, but their echoes endless.'
MOTHER THERESA

'A real friend is one who walks in when the rest of the world walks out.'
WALTER WINCHELL

'True friends, like ivy and the wall
Both stand together, and together fall.'
FRANCIS BACON

'What is a friend? A single soul in two bodies.'
ARISTOTLE

'What is the opposite of two?
A lonely me, a lonely you.'
RICHARD WILBUR

7 | ONES AND TWOS

'And in the sweetness of friendship let there be laughter, and sharing of pleasures.' KAHLIL GIBRAN

'I love you not for what you are, but for what I am when I am with you.'

ANON

'Two people holding each other up like flying buttresses.'

ERICA JONG

'Embrace me, my sweet embraceable you!

Embrace me, you irreplaceable you!

Just one look at you, my heart grew tipsy in me;

You and you alone bring out the gypsy in me.'

IRA GERSHWIN

'Love demands infinitely less than friendship.'

GEORGE JEAN NATHAN

'Love is only chatter, Friends are all that matter.'

GELETT BURGESS

'Love comes from blindness, friendship from knowledge.'

COMPTE DE BUSSY

"The language of friendship
is not words but meanings."

HENRY DAVID THOREAU

'A true friend
is the most precious
of all possessions.'
FRANCOIS, DUC DE LA ROCHEFOUCAULD

'Friends should be preferred to kings.'
VOLTAIRE

'There is no shop anywhere where one can buy friendship.'
ANTOINE DE SAINT-EXUPERY

'Friends are … God's apology for relations.'
HUGH KINGSMILL

'What is a friend?
It is a person with whom you dare to be yourself.'
FRANK CRANE

'A friend can tell you things you don't want to tell yourself.'
FRANCIS WARD WHEELER

'The great high privilege, relief and comfort of friendship
was that one had to explain nothing.'
KATHERINE MANSFIELD

'Friendship is a sheltering tree'
SAMUEL TAYLOR COLERIDGE

'A joy shared is a joy doubled' GOETHE

'Friendship consists in forgetting what one gives and remembering what one receives.'

ALEXANDRE DUMAS

'When friends meet, hearts warm.'

PROVERB

'Friendships are glued together with little kindnesses.'

MERCIA TWEEDALE

'If the while I think on thee, dear friend,
All losses are restored, and sorrows end.'
WILLIAM SHAKESPEARE

'Wherever you are it is your own friends who make your world.'
WILLIAM JAMES

'Don't walk in front of me,
I may not follow.
Don't walk behind me,
I may not lead.
Walk beside me,
And just be my friend.'
ALBERT CAMUS

'With friends at your side
no road seems too long.'
JAPANESE PROVERB

'Friendships,
like stars,
can never be replaced.' MURIEL JAMES + LOUIS SAVARY

'Holding hands at midnight
'Neath a starry sky,'
Nice work if you can get it
And you can get it if you try.'
IRA GERSHWIN

'Today you grasped the stars as they were slipping off the edge of my horizon and shook them back into the sky.'
CYNTHIA FULLER

'Friendship is the shadow of the evening
which strengthens with the setting sun of life.'
LA FONTAINE

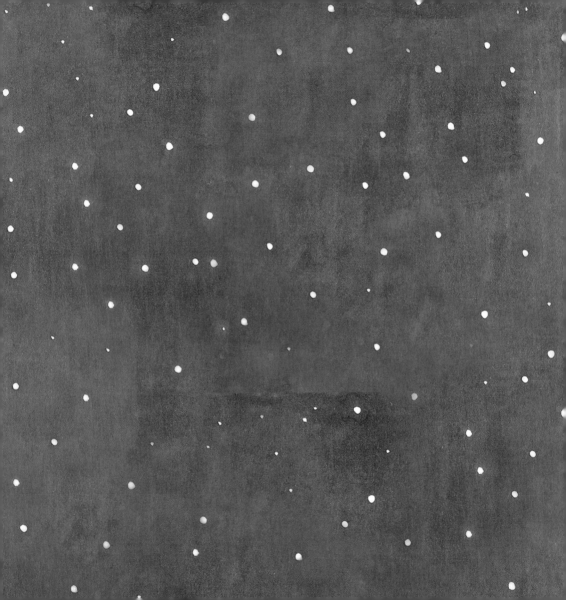